Contents

Some words are shown in bold, **like this**. You can find them in the glossary on page 23.

Many monkeys

Look at all these monkeys! There are over 200 types of monkeys in the world.

Animaths

Measuring
with Monkeys

Tracey Steffora

Raintree is an imprint of Capstone Global Library
Limited, a company incorporated in England and
Wales having its registered office at 7 Pilgrim Street,
London, EC4V 6LB – Registered company number:
6695582

www.raintreepublishers.co.uk
myorders@raintreepublishers.co.uk

Text © Capstone Global Library Limited 2014
First published in hardback in 2014
First published in paperback in 2015

The moral rights of the proprietor have been
asserted.

Edited by Daniel Nunn, Abby Colich, and Sian Smith
Designed by Joanna Hinton-Malivoire
Picture research by Elizabeth Alexander
Production by Victoria Fitzgerald
Originated by Capstone Global Library Ltd
Printed and bound in China by Leo Paper Products
Ltd

ISBN 978 1 4062 6051 9 (hardback)
17 16 15 14 13
10 9 8 7 6 5 4 3 2 1

ISBN 978 1 4062 6058 8 (paperback)
18 17 16 15
10 9 8 7 6 5 4 3 2

British Library Cataloguing in Publication Data
A full catalogue record for this book is available
from the British Library.

Acknowledgements
We would like to thank the following for permission
to reproduce photographs: Alamy p.15L (© Arco
Images GmbH); FLPA p.13 (Ingo Arndt/Minden
Pictures); Getty Images p.16 (Mint Images/Frans
Lanting); iStockphoto pp.6R (Ana Abejon), 11L (©
David Parsons), 19 (© smokyme), 20R (© Pauline
S Mills); Photoshot p.21R (Mark Bowler/NHPA);
Shutterstock pp.4, 5, 6L, 7L, 14L, 14R (© Eric Isselee),
5 (© Marina Jay), 7R (© vnlit), 8 (© Michal Ninger),
9, 10R, 11R (© ChameleonsEye), 10L (© Martin
Larcher), 15R (© Harm Kruyshaar), 18 (© Micha
Klootwijk), 20L (© Kitch Bain), 21L (© Eric Gevaert);
Superstock p.17 (imagebroker.net).

Front cover photograph of a squirrel monkey
reproduced with permission of Shutterstock (©
Marina Jay). Front cover photographs of a pygmy
marmoset, baboon, cottontop tamarin, and
front and back cover photographs of a white-
headed marmoset reproduced with permission of
Shutterstock (© Eric Isselee).

We would like to thank Elaine Bennett for her
invaluable help in the preparation of this book.

Every effort has been made to contact copyright
holders of material reproduced in this book. Any
omissions will be rectified in subsequent printings if
notice is given to the publisher.

We can **measure** to find out how things are alike and different. Let's measure some monkeys!

How tall?

This is a mandrill. Let's **measure** its **height**. Height is how tall something is.

90 cm

A mandrill is about 90 centimetres tall. That is about as tall as a 4-year-old child.

15 cm

cm stands for centimetres

The pygmy marmoset is one of the shortest monkeys. It is about 15 centimetres tall. That is about as tall as a kitten.

How long?

How long is a monkey's tail? Different monkeys have tails of different **lengths**. Monkeys use their tails for balance. This squirrel monkey can hang from its tail.

This tamarin has a tail that **measures** about 30 centimetres. That is as long as your school ruler.

This vervet monkey has a tail that can **measure** 60 centimetres long. That is twice as long as the tamarin's tail!

60 cm

30 cm

This spider monkey has a very long tail! It has a tail that can measure 90 centimetres long. That is three times as long as the tamarin's tail!

90 cm

30 cm

How far?

The long arms of the spider monkey help it swing through the trees. It can travel a great **distance**.

There are 100 centimetres in 1 metre.

It can travel 12 metres in one leap!

How heavy?

You can **weigh** things to find out how heavy they are. Monkeys can be heavy or light.

tamarin

balance

This tamarin monkey weighs about half a kilogram. That is about as heavy as a squirrel.

colobus

This colobus monkey weighs about 14 kilograms. That is about as heavy as a 3-year-old child!

How fast?

The patas monkey is the fastest monkey alive. It has long legs and can run 35 miles per hour.

Its **speed** is as fast as this savannah cat! Speed is how fast something is.

How warm?

Most monkeys live where it is warm. This saki monkey lives in the rainforest, where the **temperature** is very warm.

thermometer

This macaque can live where it is cold.

Measuring monkeys

Which monkey is taller?

60 cm

douc langur monkey

30 cm

squirrel monkey

Which monkey is heavier?

woolly monkey

titi monkey

1 kg

7 kg

kg stands for kilograms

Answers on page 22.

Monkey facts

- Monkeys live in groups. A group of monkeys is called a troop or tribe.

- Monkeys and apes are both primates. Monkeys have tails and apes do not.

- Monkeys have flexible fingers, thumbs, and toes. This helps them to hold things and use tools.

- Monkeys have excellent eyesight.

- Old World monkeys live in Africa and Asia. New World monkeys live in Central and South America.

page 21: The woolly monkey is heavier.

page 20: The douc langur monkey is taller.

Answers

Maths glossary

distance how far something is

height how tall something is

length how long something is

measure we measure to find out the size or amount of something

speed how fast something is

temperature how warm or cold something is

weigh to measure how heavy something is

Index